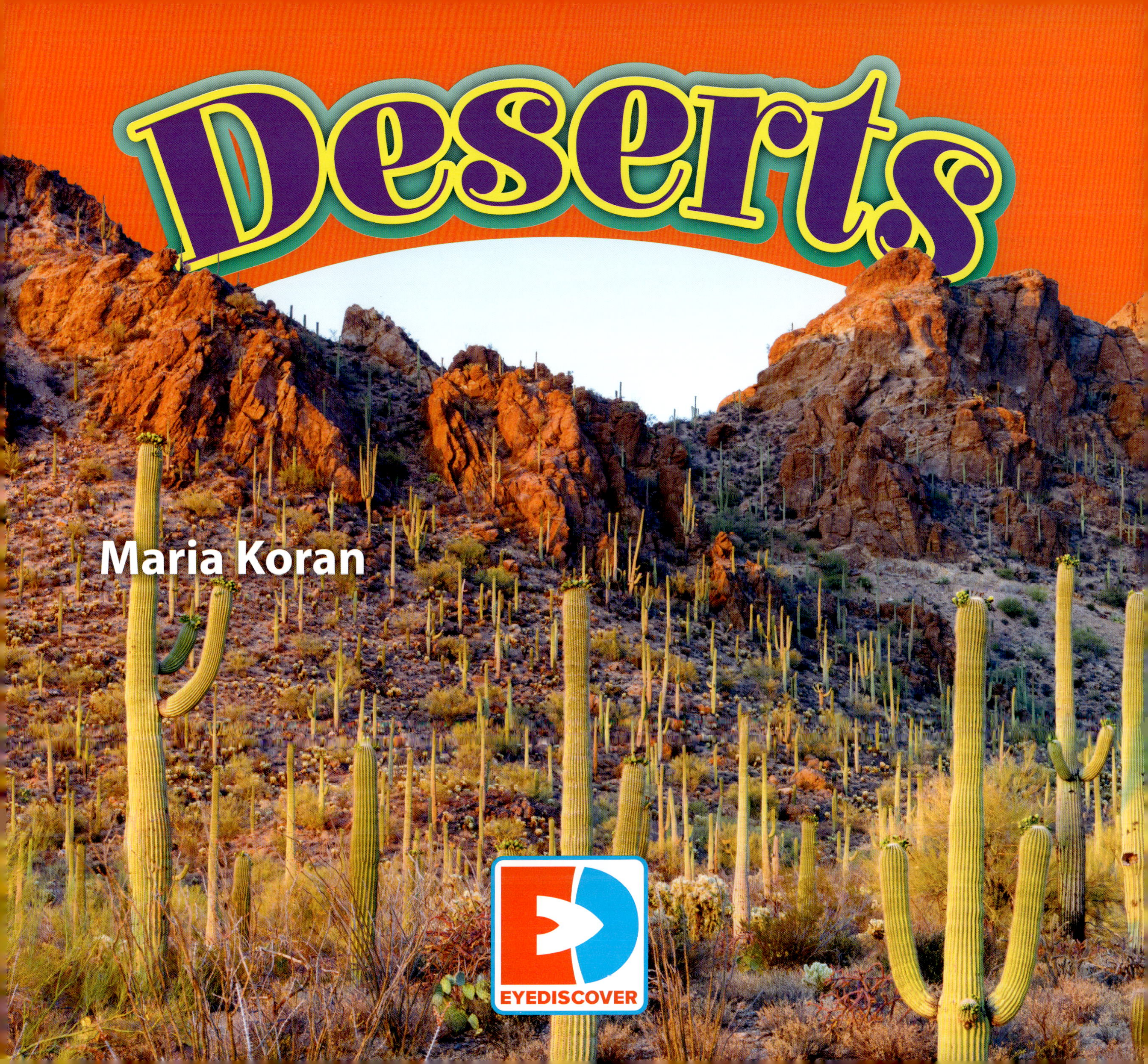
Deserts
Maria Koran
EYEDISCOVER

Go to **www.eyediscover.com** and enter this book's unique code.

BOOK CODE

AVU53346

EYEDISCOVER brings you optic readalongs that support active learning.

Published by AV² by Weigl
350 5th Avenue, 59th Floor New York, NY 10118
Website: www.eyediscover.com

Library of Congress Cataloging-in-Publication Data
available on request

ISBN 978-1-7911-0756-7 (hardcover)

Printed in Guangzhou, China
1 2 3 4 5 6 7 8 9 0 23 22 21 20 19

072019
121818

Project Coordinator: John Willis
Designer: Mandy Christiansen and Ana María Vidal

Weigl acknowledges iStock and Minden Pictures as the primary image suppliers for this title.

EYEDISCOVER provides enriched content, optimized for tablet use, that supplements and complements this book. EYEDISCOVER books strive to create inspired learning and engage young minds in a total learning experience.

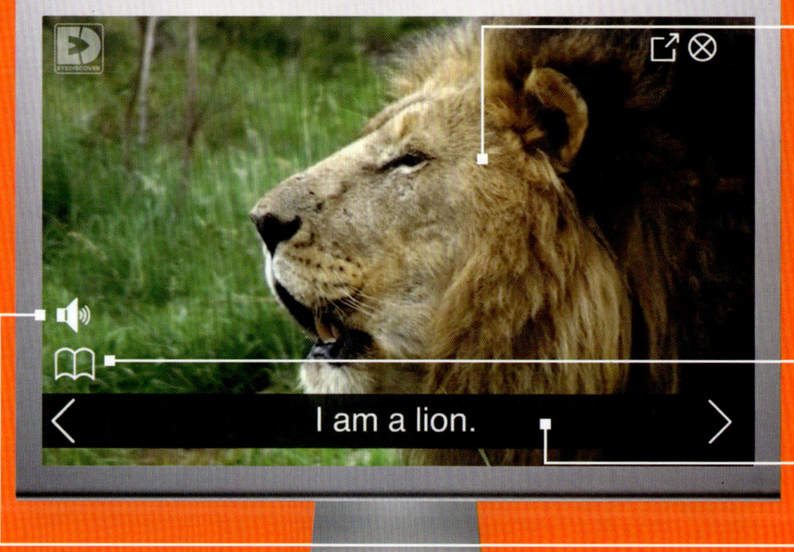

Watch
Video content brings each page to life.

Browse
Thumbnails make navigation simple.

Read
Follow along with text on the screen.

Listen
Hear each page read aloud.

Your EYEDISCOVER Optic Readalongs come alive with...

Audio
Listen to the entire book read aloud.

Video
High resolution videos turn each spread into an optic readalong.

OPTIMIZED FOR

In this book, you will learn about

- **what they are**
- **where they are**
- **what lives there**

and much more!

Deserts are places that get very little rain or snow. They never have more than 10 inches of rain or snow in a year.

6

Deserts can be hot or cold. The largest desert in the world is in Antarctica. It is very cold.

The Sahara Desert is the largest hot desert. It is in Africa. The Sahara is one of the hottest places on Earth.

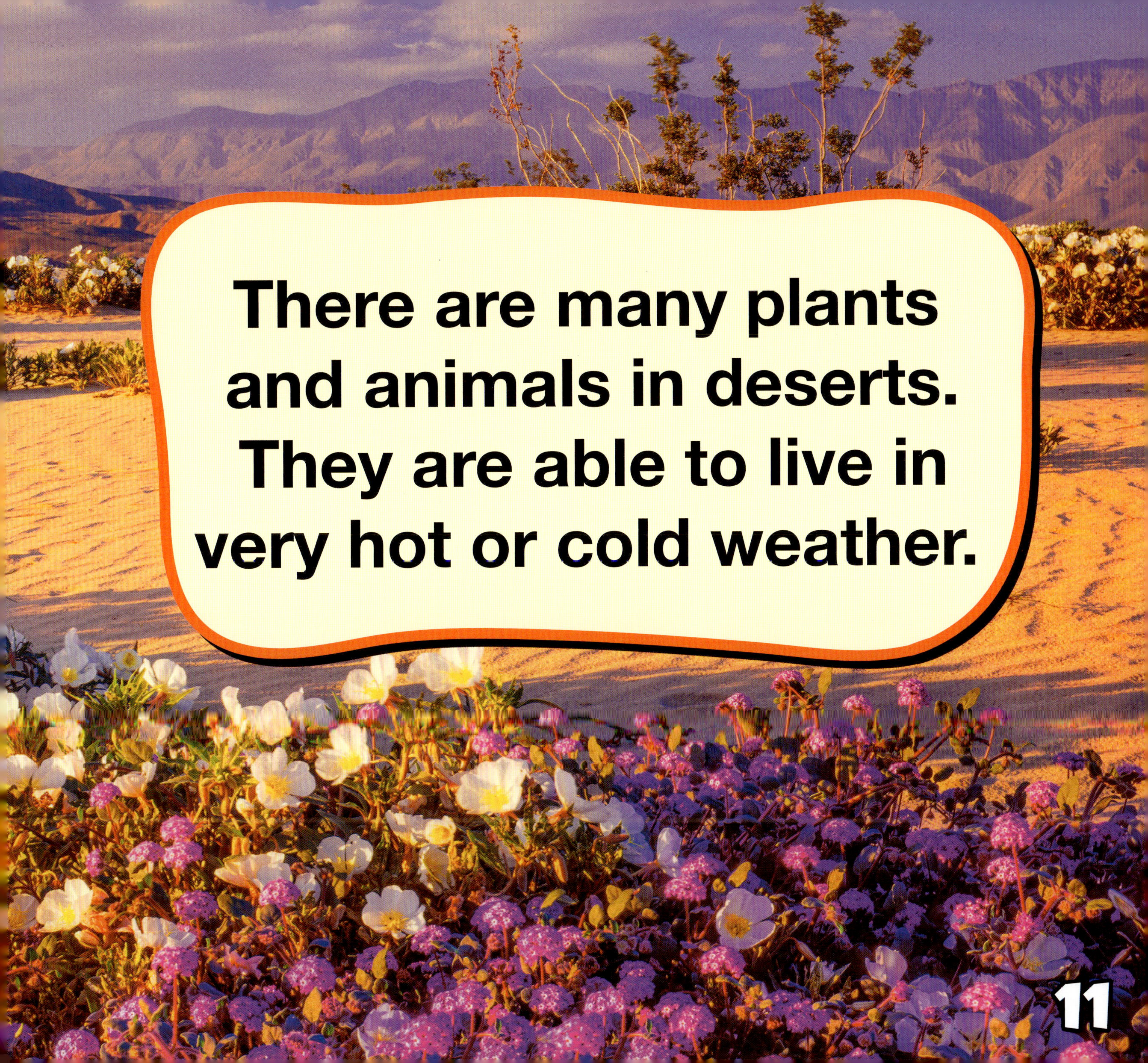

There are many plants and animals in deserts. They are able to live in very hot or cold weather.

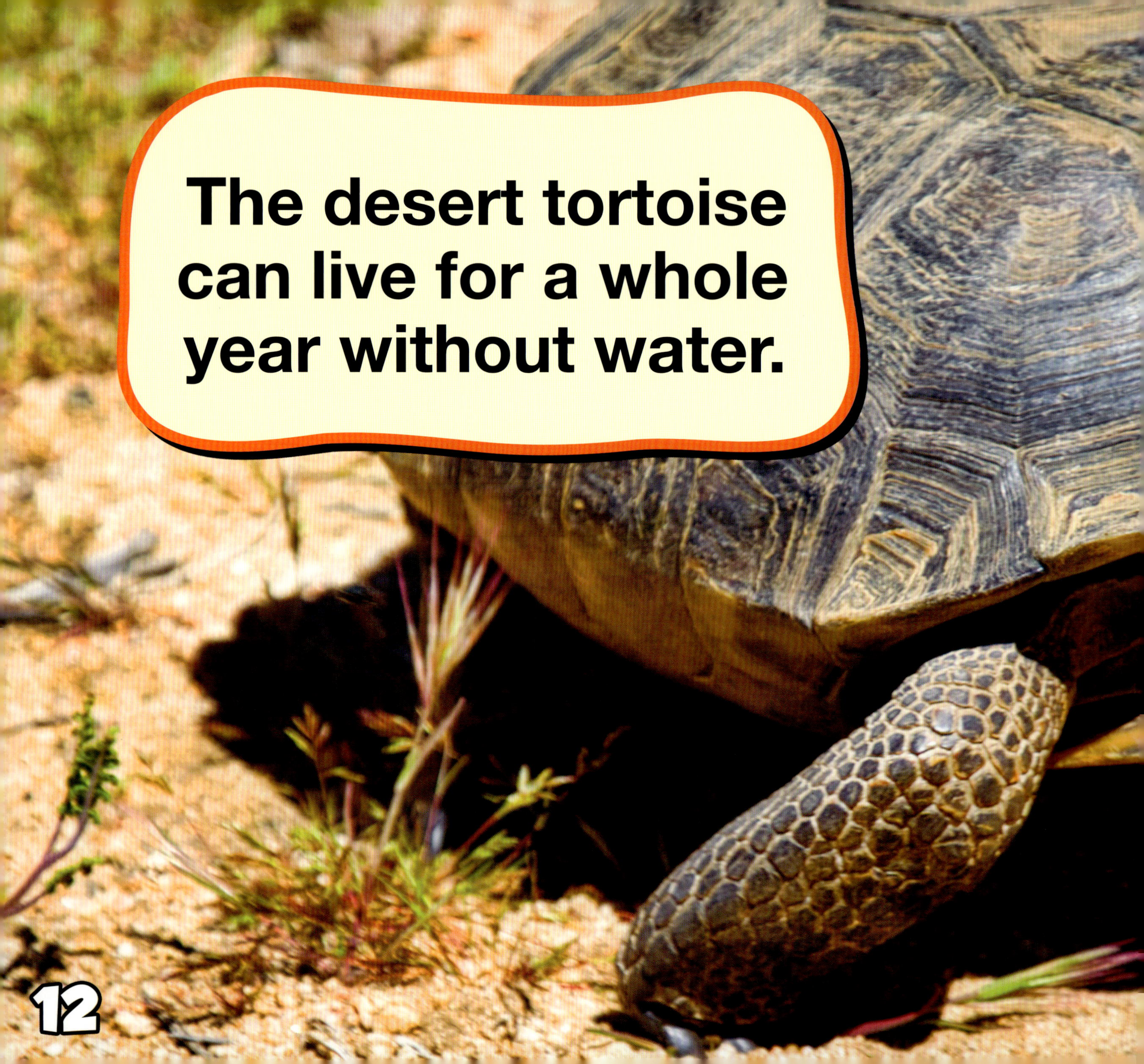
The desert tortoise can live for a whole year without water.

The most venomous snake in the world lives in the desert. One bite could kill 250,000 mice.

Many ostriches live in deserts. They can get water by eating plants instead of drinking.

Desert winds grind pebbles and sand into dust. A big wind can turn into a huge dust storm.

Deserts grow every year. This changes how plants grow and how much water we have.

The average temperature of the **Sahara Desert** is **86 degrees Fahrenheit.** (30 degrees Celsius)

An ostrich can grow to be **9 feet** tall. (2.75 meters)

A **desert tortoise** can live for up to **80 years.**

The Sahara Desert
covers 3.3 million square miles.
(8.6 million square kilometers)

Antarctica's interior
gets less than
2 inches of snow
each year. (51 millimeters)

There are four major
deserts in North America.

KEY WORDS

Research has shown that as much as 65 percent of all written material published in English is made up of 300 words. These 300 words cannot be taught using pictures or learned by sounding them out. They must be recognized by sight. This book contains 49 common sight words to help young readers improve their reading fluency and comprehension. This book also teaches young readers several important content words, such as proper nouns. These words are paired with pictures to aid in learning and improve understanding.

Page	Sight Words First Appearance
4	a, are, get, have, in, little, more, never, of, or, places, than, that, they, very, year
7	be, can, is, it, the, world
8	Earth, on, one
11	able, and, animals, live, many, plants, there, to
12	for, water, without
15	could, most
16	by
19	big, into, turn
21	changes, every, grow, how, much, this, we

Page	Content Words First Appearance
4	deserts, rain, snow
7	Antarctica
8	Africa, Sahara Desert
12	desert tortoise
15	bite, mice, snake
16	ostrich
19	dust, dust storm, pebbles, sand, winds

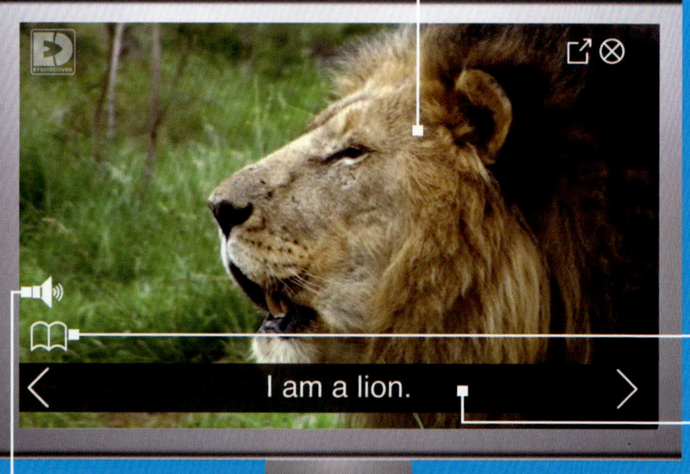

Watch
Video content brings each page to life.

Browse
Thumbnails make navigation simple.

Read
Follow along with text on the screen.

Listen
Hear each page read aloud.

Go to www.eyediscover.com and enter this book's unique code.

BOOK CODE

AVU53346